JOHN

Other books by Ron Schreiber:

(Editor) *31 New American Poets* (Hill & Wang)
Living Space (Hanging Loose Press)
Moving to a New Place (Alice James Books)
Against That Time (Alice James Books)
False Clues (Calamus Books)
Tomorrow Will Really Be Sunday (Calamus Books)

JOHN

Poems by Ron Schreiber

Hanging Loose Press/Calamus Books

This book is jointly published by Hanging Loose Press, 231
Wyckoff Street, Brooklyn, New York 11217, and Calamus
Books, P.O. Box 689, Cooper Station, New York, New York
10276.

Thanks to the following publications, in which some of these
pieces first appeared: *Hanging Loose, Radical America,
Noospaper, Redstart, New England Journal of Public Policy, Bay
Windows, RFD, Fag Rag, Agni Review, Men and Women Together
and Alone* (The Spirit That Moves Us Press).

Cover photo of John MacDonald and Kwai Lon at the cliff over-
looking Long Nook Beach, Truro, Massachusetts.

Cover design by Robert Hershon

Library of Congress Cataloging-in-Publication Data

Schreiber, Ron.
    John.

    1. AIDS (Disease)—Patients—Poetry.   I. Title.
PS3569.C52935J64   1988   811'.54   88-24689
ISBN 0-914610-63-5
ISBN 0-914610-62-7 (pbk.)

 Produced at The Print Center., Inc., 225 Varick St.,
New York, NY 10014, a non-profit facility for literary
and arts-related publications. (212) 206-8465

for Lisa Porter
for Suzanne Meglio

John MacDonald, Jr., was born in Dorchester June 10, 1951; he died in Holbrook, his parents' home, November 5, 1986. John graduated from Holbrook High School, attended Northeastern and graduated from the University of Hawaii with a degree in marine biology. He had done various things in his teens and 20s, since he was kicked out of his parents' home by his father when he was 15 (for being gay). He'd done a nightclub act in New York, cut demo records, modeled, worked as a geisha in Kyoto for three months. He worked for some years for New England Telephone Company and for many years for Winston Flowers on Newbury Street in Boston. He arranged the flowers for the 100th Anniversary of the Boston Pops. But his passions were plants—he planted whole gardens, grew orchids and camellias—and animals—he had three chows and two shih-tzus, five cats, a blue-and-gold macaw and many lesser birds and fish. He'd been cross-pollinating flowers since he was five.

The Family
Nancy Peter: John's sister.
Bobby Peter: Nancy's husband.
John MacDonald, Sr.: John's father.
Lucille MacDonald: John's mother.
Joanne MacDonald: John's aunt.
Richie and Christine MacDonald: John's younger brother and youngest sister.

The Close Friends
Suzanne Meglio: John's roommate of many years.
Lisa Gay Porter: John's home health aide.
Ron Schreiber: John's lover.

The Medical People
At Mount Auburn Hospital:
Steve Boswell: The intern who supervised John's case when he was admitted.
Nettie Tagliaferro: John's doctor.
From Cambridge Hospice:
Barbara Field: The chief hospice nurse.
Marki Webber: A hospice nurse on call.
From Massachusetts General Hospital:
Chip Schooley: John's doctor through the latter part of his illness.

The Volunteers
Gail Williams: The hospice volunteer who was with John each Wednesday.
Alba Goodwin-White: The AIDS action volunteer who came once a week.

Ron's Therapist
Richard Pillard.

January 1985; January 1986

The time between Thanksgiving and Christmas was always the busiest time for John. Customers gave parties, often large ones, and they wanted flower arrangements—perhaps smaller ones around the room, always a large centerpiece for the dining room table or the sideboard. Many customers requested John in particular, for they knew him and liked his work.

Knowing John loved plants and flowers, many of his friends thought he had the perfect job. Every winter we looked avidly at flower catalogues and we ordered well: for the garden at home in Cambridge, and the larger gardens and land at Truro. I would normally buy orchids for John on his birthday or for no occasion at all, and John brought me cut flowers or an unusual plant every week. He turned my dining room into a greenhouse in winter.

But his job was far from ideal, though John took pride in his abilities. He worked ten-hour days normally and during the holidays he often worked twelve and sometimes fourteen hours. Christmas—though he looked forward to Christmas Eve with his family—was a time of collapse rather than celebration. John usually slept until two in the afternoon. What gifts we exchanged then were perfunctory, though we could each be pleased a day or two later.

In 1985 John decided to take a vacation with me on my annual visit to my parents in Florida. First we stayed at Day's Inn in Deerfield, when we were visiting my parents. We visited orchid nurseries west of Delray Beach and bought a few exotics John could not find in the catalogues. Our own vacation began three days later, when we drove down to Flamingo, where we'd rented a housekeeping cabin in the Everglades for a week. This was John's time, when he could recover from the long hours at the flower shop, when he could sleep as long as he wanted, when there was nothing to do but see the birds and the alligators.

His blond hair grew brighter in the Florida sun; his pale skin began to acquire color. We drove together to Royal Palm and Anhingha Trail or to Mrazek Pond, where, for the first four days, wood storks and roseate spoonbills teemed in feeding frenzy. At night we walked always to Eco Pond to watch the herons come in to nest in the trees, see the anis and gallinules and coots, or spot the giant alligator in the center of the pond. One day we walked the path to Bear Lake, covering ourselves with mosquito repellent. Three times we drove into Miami to orchid nurseries or, one day, to the zoo. Soon John was rested and glowing.

—Next year, John said, we'll rent the cabin for two weeks, and we had begun to plan another winter vacation for the Caribbean, maybe my choice, Jamaica, where John had determined there were enough birds and flowers for him to like it too.

But the next year John decided instead not to come south with me, and he regretted that decision, made in September when I bought my ticket, before the Christmas rush had even begun. I went south alone in January, 1986.

When I got back, the tenth, John seemed even more tired than he was before I left, and he had acquired a shallow, dry cough, which sounded like a smoker's cough, except that John did not smoke. He wouldn't go to a doctor even after he collapsed at the subway station going into work in late January. But he agreed, finally, to go to a health stop, the day my cat Minny died, and we went there after taking her to Angell Memorial, where they began the process of cremation. He was diagnosed with bronchitis, but he only got sicker. Then, in March he agreed to go to Mount Auburn Hospital, though he wasn't pleased with going. ''They'll keep me in the hospital,'' he said, ''They won't let me come home.''

R.S.

diagnosis (4-10-86)

we'll call it an "especially
virulent form of pneumonia,"

ironically an accurate way
of saying both what it is

& what it is not. I am
stunned. what about co-

factors! I want to scream.
what about the incubation

period! Period. I have been
happy for eight and a half

years. John will be, we hope,
35 in June. June 10. two

months from now. Now.
it's a hospital bed, coughing.

vomiting unappetizing food
& red medicine that looks like

blood. especially virulent.
eight years of happiness is

more than most people get,
more than I had before. "I

have been happy & I won't be
happy anymore" is the ironic

-ally accurate way I phrase it
to myself. I'm 52. this

happiness—with this unusual &
particular man—won't happen

to me again.

the next day (4-11-86)

John is "better" today, his
eyes are brighter, he is

eating without vomiting.
from his bed you could see

the Charles in springtime
if the drapes were open.

all along the road to the
hospital forsythia bloom

& magnolia, white & sometimes
pink. tonight or tomorrow,

when I go in next, I'll
bring the orchid from his room

at home. now that he's been
diagnosed, I can come

whenever I like, regardless
of the hours. but this morning

I went in to talk with Steve
Boswell, John's intern who

has taken a special interest
in John's case. "8 months,"

Steve said, is the average, but
it could be longer or less long.

I want us to have such time
as we have together. I was

cheerful this morning.
so was John.

right now

may be the easy part. I joked
with John, "it's like a fucking

marriage: for better or for—
till death do us part." later

may be harder. except for me
& the doctors John doesn't want

anybody to know. he doesn't
want Suzanne or Nancy or his

parents to know. he doesn't
want the pity of his friends.

4-13-86

no good—these daily dated
poems. too much like a

countdown. I need now
poems for living—John is

alive & he doesn't want
to be mourned or "pitied"

—a term we've watered down
to cheap & easy sympathy,

when it used to be half of
katharsis. (the other

half is fear, or *terror.*)
angst, I told John, is

"remorse for the future,"
& I have a touch of it.

feed fish; vacuum rugs; water
plants; take pictures of

what blooms. & date these
poems as they happen,

day by day.

insight

"I knew," John said, "all the
symptoms were there." I didn't

know—unless the incubation
period is 7 years, 10 years,

it didn't seem either of us
was at risk. except for

"a bite in the bar" two years
ago, & John is sure that was

it. maybe. but I don't want
to talk about it. we don't

know how, we just know the
fact of it. I didn't know

before the tests came back,
but I'd *seen*. the first time

in the hospital, less weight,
fever over 103°. I looked at

John & saw the gaunt death
coming—in his eyes & in his

now frail body. he's "better"
this morning; they're treating him.

talking to others

it's a voice mask I put on
for all but John & Russ.

maybe not Suzanne, there's
daily contact, though she

was the first I spoke it to.
it goes: concerned, serious,

together, with a touch of ban-
ter, like an authoritative

rooster with
nothing to crow about.

4-14-86

I have trouble sleeping:
up too early; work to do;

anything to get my mind
numbed & unthoughtful; cold.

the treatment's working
but it has side effects.

like an inability to keep
food   down.

one sees the shadow, some
day things like this will

overwhelm, & that will be
it. "Next time maybe I'll

come back as a snail," John
says, "a dull life but un-

eventful." I'm tired too
today. I find the shell

appealing.

pause

a spider in my drawer among
underwear; I let it live.

—just as John cultivates
spiders in his greenhouse

(when he's home, I mean.)
let the pandas live, don't

cut down their bamboo forests.
keep them in foliage. China

is not Brazil, where whole
civilizations fall & all

their animals. or America
where death comes suddenly

or slow. I closed the drawer
though. I'm not raising spiders.

predation (4-15-86)

to open a 20-pound sack
of dry cat food, first

cut the sack with scissors.
then pour carefully into the

glass bowl, trying not to
drop pellets on the floor,

where, if they fall, after all
the cats will eat them—which

is the point anyway. not every
pellet goes into a bowl. being

eaten is the animal way—mice
for the snakes, feeder fish

(when the store has them)
for piranhas. we didn't even

load a revolver, we never spun
it, but there it was—loaded &

spinning anyway—& it hit you
squarely. guess fate's like

that sometimes, the pellet falls
on the floor, the goldfish get

torn into twenty parts.

protocols (4-16-86)

so now the test is back:
positive. no surprise.

"maybe that qualifies you
for a protocol," I say.

I'll get disability,"
John says. either way

he's qualified. he'll be
home in two days—medication

oral. Dr. Tagliaferro
mentioned "control groups,"

an easier term than "protocol."
but John doesn't like the

idea of being used as a
guinea pig. or the possible

side effects, which, he says,
could kill him. but what

if he says yes? is hope
a chimera without even a

gold ring in its nose?
or is it possibility, slowly

creeping through a crack in
the stone door, wriggling

its wormy body into a
kind of life?

your life (4-18-86)

right now it's all I care about
& you're going to lose it

(wrong head, I know, but it's
late & I'm scared & tired).

first there's your health: I
want you to have it. you were

exhausted & sun-dazed when I
brought you back from the hospital

—after stopping to get your drugs—
& you were sleeping when I called

downstairs just now. I am tired
beyond anything my body tells me

is fatigue. & when you're sick,

when I look into your tired, lovely
eyes, I want you well. right now

I'm trying to find the railroad cap
I lost on the long flight wait

in Florida last winter, when I was
there & you were home & healthy,

& put it on my head firm & screw it
on. I want you to get back your

health or at least its shimmering
surface. right now.

Sunday morning (4-20-86)

John got out of the hospital Thursday morning. We did not know whether he'd be able to leave or not, since his white blood count was low Wednesday night, and they had to get the results of another blood test Thursday morning. OK—so we left.

The sun hurt his eyes coming home. We stopped at the pharmacy to pick up his drugs, and they were expensive: over $100. for four prescriptions. When we got home he was very tired and he was nauseous again.

When John came upstairs Friday morning, I was momentarily elated: he must be better, I thought. But that was not the case: his fever had returned, the rash had begun again, and he was very weak. While he lay on my bed, I kept trying to reach his doctor, who was not in yet. The intern, Steve Boswell, called about an hour later, and told me to bring John in. Then, as John was walking down the stairs, the phone rang again, and this time it was Nettie Tagliaferro, his doctor, and she said to bring John in.

He was very bad when we reached the emergency room, and I was unwilling to leave until I thought he would be all right. I left about 11, and went into work, as I had done the day before. This time they will keep John two weeks, although apparently the new drug they are using could be administered on an out-patient basis; we would come in for an hour every day. But John does not want that, and I don't think I could stand it.

When I talked to Steve Friday afternoon, he asked me how I was doing. —Not very well, I said, though also, —as well as can be expected, I think. I asked Steve whether it was life-threatening this time, and Steve said no, not this time. We talked a little about protocols. —I want to be with John when he dies, I said. Steve assured me that they would call me right away if anything should happen.

But this time they think it will be all right. We don't know yet what the side effects of this drug will be. Probably we will have to wait ten days and then find out. So far, whenever there are potential side effects, John gets them. They just have to keep trying new drugs. Probably the rash, though, is not a side effect (though it could be), but another opportunistic disease.

Last night I slept nine hours, from 9 to 6; I had also fallen asleep in the afternoon. I am still tired this morning. I hope I can use each weekend to recuperate, for my job is very busy. This is only the second day of a three-day weekend, so I can't tell yet whether the weekend will be long enough. I may have to live with this fatigue. But that is not so difficult as what John has to do, which is to live with his various illnesses and side effects as long as he wants to, as long as he can.

back in (4-21-86)

Saturday I waited for the plumber
all morning, & he came at one, but

I'd left the door open & visited
you in the morning. yesterday I

came by twice, & in between got
potting soil so Sue could put up

the plants we'd ordered & dog &
cat food for your larger animals.

today I'm waiting for the extermi
-nator & trying to read the book

I'm teaching tomorrow. when I come
by this afternoon it will be masks

& gloves & paper gown again, not
because you're contagious but for

fear of what I might bring in,
your white count down again.

we'll relate to each other as if
you're living, we said, but this

way it's hard: you in the hospital
& very sick, your whole attention

focused on your body & your illness.
sure, you're living, but I get left

out of the equation, except for job
& chores, the structure of routine,

& thinking of you, thinking of you
all the time.

moving towards memory (4-22-86)

what scares me most is that the
virus often goes to the brain.

such a sharp mind, tongue like
a razor, but beard now unshaved

for weeks. then, yesterday (so
soon), John could not remember

the end of a sentence he'd begun.
at noon, when he seemed to be

miserable from the blood samples
of the morning; in the evening

when his left arm was swollen.
it's happening fast, but this

part is—now at least—more
gentle than I'd expected, like

waking from calm sleep too
early to be able to piece

sentences together, or remember
what it was one wanted to say.

4-23-86

Seizures began. The red spots on John's skin grew larger and covered his whole body. His fever went up to 104 and stayed there. The only sounds John made were continual moans.

They had placed under John a pad hooked up to a large, primitive machine that produced cold, the best device they knew to lower his fever. When I came in in the morning, Nettie and Steve insisted I call his parents, and when they came, John's father asked me outright: "Is it AIDS?" "Yes," I told him and I began to cry. We talked about life support decisions (negative—for John had already spoken about that) and about arrangements for burial, and a memorial service at the parents' Baptist church. Steve Boswell came downstairs and talked with the parents and, again, with me.

Richie, John's brother, came and could not stop crying. He spent the night in the lounge. Steve Boswell stayed with John all night. When I came back the next morning, nothing had changed. John continued to moan and thrash; he was still hooked up to the machine, but his fever had not gone down. That evening I went to my men's group and told them for the first time, though Peter already knew. "John has AIDS," I said, "and he's dying right now."

I went back to the hospital after the group, and a nurse had just disconnected the machine. John's fever had gone down. I saw Steve. "Thanks," I said, "you've been wonderful."

deathwatch (4-24-86)

I've unpacked the plant I
could not unpack last night.

I've watered it, watched the
cats tear through the paper,

though they can't read. I
watered other plants. I

wrote my parents to tell them
the latest about John: that

he had seizures Tuesday, his
parents came to the hospital

& that we've made all the
final decisions. that John

seemed to feel at ease with
dying as if it were a natural

process he'd known many times
with animals (Vlasta died in

his arms). John told me,
shortly after we met, that

I'd outlive him. it's just
that neither of us thought

it would be so soon.

the valley of death (4-25-86)

John didn't die. he hasn't
died yet. but he's only

rarely coherent, we're
thankful for a smile, a

shard of conversation.
when he screams "no no no

no no" "go home," we are
glad that he has his voice

back & says actual words
rather than moans. when

he claws at his chest, we
say, "he's trying to use

his hands." today he
may be better, longer

moments of attempted speech.
today he may not

be better. we don't know:
day to day, hour to hour.

it will be short or longer.
his brain will work

or it won't.

4-25-86

I visited John in the hospital
& he was answering the nurse's

questions. "where are you?"
"Holbrook." not right. she

asks again. "home." still
not right. John can't turn

his head to the left, so he
didn't see me, probably didn't

recognize my voice. I came
home. called Janet at work;

called Russ; spoke to Suzanne.
did a laundry. read the utility

meters & called the company.
when I was folding the laundry,

the mail came, a white envelope,
gray border, from the Netherlands:

"mijn allerliefste Henk, onze
lieve pappa," Hendrick Nicolaas

de Ruijg, "op de leeftijd van
49 jaar." if one lives long

enough, the people he knows
begin to die. I can't stand it.

finches

"look!" John said, pointing
to the far wall at the big

machine that had kept him
cool for two days, "finches!"

his voice was not back yet,
only an excited whisper.

"there aren't any finches,"
I said. "yes there are!"

John said, "call the nurse."
I called the nurse, who came

& said, "no, I don't see the
finches." "oh," said John.

"but you used to have finches
at home," I said, & John smiled,

remembering, & then looking at
the machine again & describing

in detail the beautiful
finches that weren't there.

John was alone

in the room when I came to visit.
he was talking to his boss Maynard

about giving Kwai Lon to an old
Chinese woman after he died.

he was entirely lucid.
I stood by the bed & listened.

John's eyes were open maniacally
& he stared through me.

finally I interrupted: "I'm
not Maynard," I said. John

was irritated: "I know you're
not Maynard, you're Ron, but

I'm talking to Maynard."
& he continued to make practical

plans for Kwai, who was sad & quiet
at home because John wasn't there.

preparing to visit (4-30-86)

I've been up an hour but I'm
still not dressed. I forget

to look at myself in the mirror
to see if I'm losing weight or

putting more on. you're in
restraints, tied to your bed,

so you won't fall out or crawl
out to look for baby alligators

or hurt yourself. two days ago
your voice was clear & loud,

yesterday it was barely audible.
all this will change one way or

another. I don't look forward
to anything. I remember to shower.

I put on my clothes.

back (4-30-86)

"he's back," I say to Suzanne
when she comes in the room.

talking normally, but weak,
feet in pain—I massage his

calves, speak with him; he
doesn't remember much, but

making a movie in delirium,
being eaten by rats. He'd

been raped, he tells me, by
a large man in an alley behind

Newbury Street or in Harvard
Square, but this is not the

dream; it's what he tells me
in his returned state of

"normalcy" or weakness or
still in danger & maybe

there's something else or
maybe not but it doesn't

make a difference because
I thought I'd never speak

with him again.

memory exercises

"do you remember your dogs?"
I ask. John smiles.

"there's Jadey...and Lili,"
he says slowly. "What about

your chows?" "do I have *chows*?"
John asks. "yes," I say,

"there's Kwai Lon." he smiles
from ear to ear. "Kwai Lon,"

he says. "& Sushi & Ching,"
I say, but John can't remember.

"Jenny," John says. "Jenny died,"
I tell him, & John looks sad.

"what about your cats?"I ask.
"oh," John smiles. "there's

Nefer & Tauri...." "what about
Mandy?" I say. John looks puzzled.

"Suzanne's white cat," I add,
& John remembers. "& Isis & Onyx,"

I say, but John can't remember them.
"do you remember my Abyssinians?"

I ask, & John's eyes open wide:
"you have *Abies*?" he says. he

remembers Mijnsje & Rimpy, my old
cats who died, but not Vlasta, my

first Aby, who died in his arms,
or Minny, who died the day we first

took John to a doctor, or Teri
& the Grinks, who will keep me

company when John is gone.

the long haul (5-6-86)

''long'' means he didn't
die last week, it means

maybe he won't die this
week either, or maybe not

the next. it refers to an
unspecified length of time

in which anything can happen,
horribly. that he didn't

die last week means we get
to go through it again.

mother's day (5-11-86)

"he's stable, " is all I can answer
"weaker yesterday," "a little stronger

this morning." it's mother's day,
and my own mother calls me.

they're going out for brunch.
I'm visiting the hospital, buying

food for John's dogs & cats, food
for my cats, watching the game

between the Sixers & the Bucks,
trying to finish reading journals

from students, wondering, as the day
goes on, whether I'll visit again

this evening—with Suzanne, John's
parents probably,who knows what

cousin or uncle is already there. I
need time alone with you,

you need that time from me, where
we're easy & simple together, hoping

that you'll get out of the hospital
to stay next time—for a few weeks or

months. "are you afraid of dying?"
I ask, and you answer, "no."

5-18-86

your arms & legs are shrunken
mush, the muscles gone—but

already—as you begin to eat—
the arms start to come back.

you have a walker for your legs
& you walk to the toilet

across your room. except for
the weekend (which is now) you

have help: a woman from PT.
now the floor is badly under-

staffed. you're on your own
—with visits from your parents,

Nancy, Suzanne. I come twice
a day, my routine pegged to your

"recovery." at home I'm getting
prepared: yesterday I cleaned

the guest room, where you'll
stay; this morning I've raised

the storms & put the screens in.
the cats huddle at the windows &

listen to birds they haven't
heard all winter. the Easter

cactus blooms in your new room,
if you do indeed "recover" this week:

bright, gaudy red flowers, full
in the sun, as wide as an arm.

summer (5-19-86)

80, in the. . . .I've
moved the orchids & camellias

to the porch, with Suzanne's
help (she tied the window

boxes to the railing, helped
me sweep)—lucky I got a haircut

this morning, at the corner
(the new no appointment shop

in the changing neighborhood)
—& put the air conditioner

in my study window, upside down
first, till I realized it was

. . . . they're John's plants;
so's the wisteria blooming in

the yard the first time in
two years—Jennie buried under

it, Mijnsje too, the first
animals to die. . . . his plants,

but he's still in the hospital,
still coughing, a little fever

this morning, too weak to bathe,
though I was staying to help him

. . . . his plants. usually he
moves them to the porch himself.

home (5-26-86)

All the logistics went wrong. I thought John would come home next week, but when I got to the hospital conference (nurses, PT therapist, doctor), it had been decided tomorrow. I had planned to go to the Cape, to change the bank accounts that had to be changed if John was to get Medicaid. I would plant the flowers, small trees, and raspberries we'd ordered & finally see the Cape & finally rest. But it all changed.

Plans were made for Friday: the ambulance would pick John up between 5 & 6, the oxygen people would deliver the tank between 3 & 6, the visiting nurse would come Saturday, & the home health worker would begin, 5 hours a day, on Monday, which is Memorial Day.

Nothing worked as planned. By 6 John was not home. (The day shift, without its regular nurse, had forgotten to order the ambulance.) By 6 the oxygen had not arrived (deliveries were running 3 hours late). My phone was not working & we need the phone: to call John's parents or his sister or his aunt; to call the doctor when we need to page her. My car lights were on, & I couldn't turn them off or start the car.

John came home at 8; the oxygen arrived simultaneously. Saturday morning it took a phone repairman two hours to fix the phone. I'll have to take my car to the garage (but I don't need to visit the hospital twice a day). The home health worker lives in Dorchester & claims he does not know how to get to Cambridge.

(Friday night I was hysterical, the worst I've been. I asked Suzanne to stay upstairs with me until John got home. Neither of us ate dinner. Thursday night Mark ran wires to hook up an extension phone for John's room. Saturday Linda took me to the pet store to get food for the animals & to a mattress store to get a high mattress for John's bed. Today Suzanne came up & talked with John. Yesterday John's parents, his aunt Joanne & his kid sister visited. Tomorrow Suzanne will stay home with John so I can go to work.)

John is better. His spirits are better, his energy seems better. His little blind shih-tzu Jadey is with him, my cats haunt his bed & often sleep there. The oxygen works. John does not eat enough, but he eats, & he drinks Ensure regularly. He takes his pills. He has not been vomiting. His fever is down. He coughs, but he has medicine to take for the cough.

Suzanne (6-4-86)

feeds the chows & shih-
tzus, the five cats, the

macaw, the rabbit, the
ordinary fish & the piranhas

(feeder fish), also the snakes
(live mice). she keeps the

apartment clean, does the laundry.
that's just the start.

for instance, Monday (when
I was on the Cape), she watched

John's seizure & called the
ambulance, got him to the

hospital, stayed till 2,
visited, left notes on both

my doors—to see her before
I went upstairs (where John

was gone). her week's vacation
is nearly gone, & she's exhausted.

no rest with this, just
strategies. without her I'd

be the other side of exhaustion
now. John might be dead.

Great Meadow (6-7-86)

the rain stopped & turned to mist.
"the geese," a blond woman said,

"have gone over to the other pond,
so you've got to walk a ways."

I've walked enough. John's at home,
in bed; his parents are visiting,

& I need my own space. which is
here this grey afternoon.

"a mini-Truro," I told John before
I left; the red-winged blackbirds

I'm used to seeing at the bend of
the Little Pamet are here in June.

in a "normal" June I'd be in Truro,
but that's two hours away, & two

hours is the most time I'll leave
you alone, though right now your

mother's with you & she could care
for you if something happened, till

I got back & did whatever it was
I had to do.

home care

The home health care worker was supposed to come Memorial Day, but he begged off the case. Cambridge VNA told me they were having a difficult time finding persons who would work with AIDS patients, though one day they sent over a woman who tended to John efficiently & cleaned his room & the kitchen. John liked her, even though she continually talked about God. Looking at the kitchen floor, she said to me, "What you need is a homemaker, not a health care worker."

Barbara Sullivan, the VNA nurse, asked me over the phone: "Do you mean to say that you can't go to work unless you have a home health aide?" "That's exactly what I mean," I said. But John was being transferred from Visiting Nurses to Hospice, and somehow Hospice came through, remarkably. From no help at all (Suzanne had used up her vacation; she could not take more days off from work), we suddenly had Lisa, who had cared for AIDS patients in Berkeley. Lisa had been trying to work with AIDS patients for the last two months before she was given John's case.

Lisa first came when I was in Truro, and then for only a day, since John was readmitted to the hospital.

Lisa (6-8-86)

is not a homemaker, she
is in fact about as neat

& tidy as I, which is not
slobful but an attitude of

having something better
to do than clean. her

strategy is to come as a
friend, & she got sucked in:

John prefers women to men.
she is also an amazing young

woman: competent, articulate,
gay (that's her middle name),

political, even one with a
wry or robust (alternating)

sense of humor, capable of
caring for persons she did

not know a month earlier.
& she'd worked with AIDS

patients not in Boston,
where we all defer to doctors,

but in the Bay Area, where
a community has learned to

take care of one another.
she became my friend.

she became John's friend.

6-9-86

I don't know whether I
can do my job. you've been

sleeping, for four hours
already. but now Lisa's

here, five hours a day
(my work hours). your

doctor's withdrawing from
your case—frustrated by

being able to do nothing
maybe, maybe homophobic,

but she's not helpful.
so it's you & me & Lisa

& hospice, & I'm going
back to work, though my

real job has been with you:
when you wake disoriented

I get up to find your pill
& the tube you put in your

nose for oxygen. last night
you fell in the bathroom &

I didn't hear you, my sleep
tuned only for your cough

& your helplessness in sleep.
now you're sleeping. Lisa's

coming. I'm going to work.

"happy birthday" (6-10-86)

a month ago I didn't know
I'd get to say that, but now

you're here. you're home.
you're 35.

you're living.

6-11-86

you looked as if you were starting
to have another seizure, & we don't

want you to. when I heard your dogs
bark downstairs, I called Suzanne, who

fed them & came up. I had a hard time
getting you to put on the oxygen; you

hated the tube, frowned at it, you were
worried about my cats—had they got out?

Alba rang the bell, I let her in.
I brought a cold cloth for your head.

Suzanne held you & talked to you
as if you were a little child.

I called the doctors, who were not in,
but talked with their backups about

changing your medication. & this time
you fought it off. "I'd rather die here,"

you said, "than go to the hospital again."
"happy birthday," I wrote you yesterday

before I went to work. today you're
exhausted. me too.

junkies, niggers, & queers

oh it's junkies, niggers & queers
& the men don't care. some

doctors care, some nurses, some
lovers & families & friends.

some doctors flee, & nurses.
some families turn their backs.

some lovers run away.
but the men who run things

—who appropriate money or
preach from pulpits—don't

see themselves at risk.
if it's old white veterans,

the money pours in.
if it's women, it may be

dismissed as "all in the mind."
but this time it's the

official scum, & they just
don't care about junkies

& niggers & queers.

midsummer's day, 1986

Jadey Catwater laps at the bowl.
Jadey Shitter has to be carried outside

—because she's small, because she's blind.
the cats put on a floor show, air show,

sniff-&-watch show, because it's early,
because Jadey Catwater is lapping at

their bowl, because she's barking on
the back porch. this is as long as it gets.

John lies in bed, better than yesterday when
his brain waves sparked & he coughed & slept.

I prepare for a cool day in Cambridge &
Boston, on foot. Jadey Catwater is back

in bed with John. I lap at my coffee,
which is bitter from the old pot.

the sun is shining & it's cold.

better (6-25-86)

"I just woke up," you say.
I woke up two hours ago to

your falling: a broken glass
on the floor; helped you back

to bed; wiped the floor free
of glass & water—I'm still

shaky. I'll be shaky at least
until I go out to the subway,

the dentist, the gay bookstore,
Boston Garden to get a refund

on what could have been the
seventh game of the finals.

you're stable now: no
seizures for days, no greater

weakness (or strength), no
vomiting or fever spikes.

but still in bed, drinking
juice on your back ("sit up,"

I order, & you say, "I just
woke up"). what is normal for you

often leaves me shaking, &
I adjust & try to flow with

the changes of your illness.
we call this "stable," & I guess

—on a scale of health to death—
it is relatively calm.

"it's like living in a

bucket," you said. then
we both cried together—

maybe the first time for
either of us. now another

mini-seizure; fatigue;
awaking. no progress.

no regression either.
just the same except we

don't know what will happen,
when the bucket will leak

& the water run out.

canaries

when I came home, Suzanne was
sitting upstairs with John.

my cats—Teri, Tanan, and
Rimpy—were sitting quietly

around the room, their ears
up, the large eyes narrowed

to slits, looking at the top
of the television, where Suzanne

had brought a cage of canaries.
"what are those doing here?" I

said. "John wants them," she said.
"I want them," John said.

(—we want them, the cats
were saying in their

alert & silent watch.)

visiting (6-28-86)

Linda calls to see whether
it would be a good day to visit.

"had you called yesterday,"
I tell her, "it would have been

fine." but John coughed
all night last night. at

6 this morning Marki told me
over the phone that codeine

was a cough suppressant, which
I hadn't known. & I'm just back

from buying Robitussin, which
doesn't work. we don't know

—from day to day, hour to hour—
what will happen next.

"more of the same," Barbara thinks,
only John will get weaker.

some day soon I may have to
ask him whether he wants us

to call an ambulance or whether
we should let him die at home.

fever (6-30-86)

suddenly weaker: all morning
he eats practically nothing,

coughs less, but now his fever
—which was normal for 2 weeks—

is starting to go up. I feel
his forehead & Lisa takes his

temp: 100.6. maybe it's still
going up, maybe up & down.

it's the last day of June.
he'll make July, just as

twenty days ago he made his
thirty-fifth birthday.

August? our ninth anniversary?
I don't even know where he'll be

tomorrow: sick in bed in the
next room or back in the hospital

again.

7-2-86

it's in the hands of doctors,
& they all wear gloves.

another seizure today:
brief, one minute or two,

no more. "I don't want
to do this anymore."

(neither do I.)

the fourth of July, 1986

John's thin, hacking cough had returned. His seizures seemed to be returning. For the cough I got up at least twice a night to give John medicine & get him to put on his oxygen, which seemed to help a little. I felt sure that the pneumonia was back.

Dr. Tagliaferro, whom I was calling regularly in my anxiety, told me to stop calling her and to work through Barbara. But I called Chip Schooley at Massachusetts General Hospital, since Schooley was a specialist who worked with AIDS and AIDS patients. He was able to give me information, which made me feel a little more knowledgeable.

The second time I called Dr. Schooley happened to be July 3, and I asked him, if things with John got worse, whether I could admit him to Mass General. Although the hospital was full, Chip told me that I could.

Shortly after Lisa left the afternoon of the third, John began getting restless, as if seizures were about to come again. I called Marki, who was on call for hospice, to warn her: "I may be calling you to come out in the middle of the night." Suzanne came up for two hours after coming home from work, but John began to seem calmer and she went downstairs at nine. Just after she left, John began getting restless again, and less coherent. By the time I called Suzanne for help at 11, John was sitting up and trying to get out of bed. When I tried to give him the oxygen tube, he threw it at me. He was coughing, his eyes were glazed, and he was talking very loud. Suzanne and I had to restrain him physically. Suzanne talked softly to him, I shouted at him, and John screamed at us both. I called Marki.

We could not control John except by being there, every minute. I had decided to put John back in the hospital. John was furious with me: I had promised he would not go back to the hospital again, and I was breaking my promise. Marki paved the way: she called Mount Auburn, which had room; and Mass General, which did not. But the second reason for admission was to change doctors. How do I get John into Mass General? I asked Marki. "Just present him," she said.

When the ambulance men arrived, they asked, "Mount Auburn?" for they had transported John twice before. I hesitated, then looked at Marki, who smiled. "Mass General," I said. I took a caffeine pill to keep me awake and, at 3:30 in the morning, got into the ambulance with John.

When we got to Mass General, they did not want to admit him. The admitting physician wanted me to put John back into an ambulance and take him to Mount Auburn, where doctors were already familiar with his case. I argued with the doctor and kept telling her that Dr. Schooley said he could be admitted. Finally, she came into the room and said, "You lucked out; Dr. Schooley's on the phone." I talked with him.

John was admitted, though a room wouldn't be ready until 3 that afternoon. When Schooley arrived at 6 a.m., he sent me to Mount Auburn to get John's X-rays. When I got back, in my own car this time, Schooley compared the old X-rays with the new ones Mass General had just taken. "There's a new spot," he said.

When I got home, I called Lisa and told her what had happened. She said she and April would visit John, which they did. I went downstairs and told Suzanne that everything was all right. I called John's parents.

John spent a week in Mass General, and then he came home. His seizure medication was changed to include phenolbarbitol, and he did not have any more seizures. They had taken him off oxygen in the hospital, and he remained off oxygen when he came home, though the tank still stood—if needed—at his bedside. Barbara came for another week to administer the rest of the pentamadine, and we managed, despite its toxic effects, to get in twelve of the prescribed fourteen treatments.

back home (7-12-86)

no lyrics in this. take in-
dependence & turn it to bed-

ridden. take vivacity &
turn it to drowsiness.

turn energy into bedpans.
turn strong legs into mush.

one looks for dignity & sees
sparks of dignity, flickering.

towards "out." towards not
at all. one looks for dignity

in oneself & finds a kind of
pleasure in not hating shitwork.

in being used to it. but some-
times it's real shit—what I

pour from pan to toilet.
it takes the ability to move

my own legs out of bed in the
middle of the night when John

coughs. he's home now:
the second day, after a week in

the hospital. he's glad
to be home. he has his small

dog with him. the goldfish
I bought him have died, the

fishtank's empty. I'm beginning
to feel emptier & emptier too,

& soon—this month or next—
it will all be drained.

7-14-86

whoever comes—Lisa five
days a week from 9 till 2;

his parents or aunt on
Sundays; Suzanne just now

from downstairs; Nancy & Bobby
on Saturdays; Nancy & Joanne

on Wednesday night; Gail
on Wednesday afternoon;

Alba on Thursday night;
even Barbara, who gives him

the pentamadine, whatever
its effects—whoever comes

is bonus, a kind of enter-
tainment almost as if there's

still time for me to order
rhapis palms, for Nancy &

Bobby to bring new fish for
the tanks, for John to see

the plants & fish. whoever
visits brings John cheer &

almost a kind of hope. I'm
here every day & night &

see him tired, coughing,
getting weaker. I'm his

daily life, of which there
isn't much more.

7-22-86

now he's full of shit—
all night long, even after

an hour-long enema. side
effects? like the rash?

we're done with pentamadine
now, probably forever. it's

too strong. a "cure worse
than the disease," though

nothing is quite worse.
Jadey died yesterday:

I must have left her on the
porch & she fell two flights,

a gash in her stomach. when
we got her to the hospital

they told us she was sick &
dying anyway. so I didn't quite

kill her myself with my negli-
gence, though it felt that way

driving with Sue to Angell, me
crying all the way. they put

her down; I was touching her.
that's how John's disease began:

our driving to the animal hospital
to have my cat Minny put down.

I'm accumulating bronze urns
with ashes in them. John's feet

are swollen; he has a rash on
his legs; & now he's shitting.

all this is still his "good time."
the worst hasn't happened yet.

time (7-24-86)

if the spirit dog is dead,
John's body is also dying.

a new shih-tzu puppy will
not bring him back to life.

now the mind—called "spirit,"
called "soul"—is beginning

to go. the body is further
weakening. if the spirit

dog is dead— & Jadey died—
John's spirit (this body,

this time around) is be-
ginning to seek its release:

little eating, little urge
for cleanliness (it's still

early, if July is early
& August is very late).

Monday (7-28-86)

Friday I got John a new
(beautiful, he said) shi-

tzu puppy. John's eyes
grew huge; he smiled.

suddenly he's happy. we
hoped the dog (Jadey's ashes

will be buried with John's)
would give him energy, some-

thing to live for in that
single room. instead she

brings him pleasure, which
will have to be enough.

three smooth weeks (8-18-86)

it's been an "easy" time, no
seizures, no horrible coughing

at night, & suddenly—three
weekends ago—he began to get

his appetite back. weird:
pizza, spaghetti & meatballs;

ice cream; cookies; lox &
bagels; lobster. & began

gaining weight, the first
time in all these months

he's grown stronger. & then
it tapers off, back

drip by drip
to the usual direction:

more sleep, not so much
appetite (though, when it comes,

it's for the same weird things),
& the new weight (hardly heft)

drifts away again, to that
frail body he keeps in bed

all day long, where I look in
throughout the day & often

at night & don't (he reminds me)
talk with him enough.

countdown (8-27-86)

the pain in the center of
John's chest is not his heart.

it's only heartburn, exacerbated
by his general weakness: his

matchstick legs, his coughing
(again), his inability to eat.

the pills hurt him when he
swallows. this is not another

opportunistic disease, but only
something common that hurts him

more than it would hurt someone else.
it's difficult to get him to sit up

at all, or to drink his Ensure.
last night John & I nearly fought

—I called Suzanne to step in
between us. (I can't stand

the first day of something
new & painful). "are you prepared,"

Lisa asked me, "for John to die
in September?" (she had been

crying when she realized he would
die soon.) until she asked,

I would have said "yes."
but I said "no." no. I'll

never be prepared.

slope (8-29-86)

now it goes from bed
pan to pad, & I learn

to wear rubber gloves.
John's weaker. but his

mind is still sharp, he
still plans to live till

winter or even spring,
which he won't.

we cried together this
morning, when my anger

turned from its mask, when
John started crying.

"I don't want to cause you
pain," he said—which he

does whenever he hurts &
I can't help him.

Labor Day, 1986

here's what I have to do on Labor Day weekend
to prepare for the first day of classes, which is tomorrow:

water the plants; feed the cats & make sure the little
dog has food & water; give John his pills three times today

& his Ensure, without which he would get still weaker;
fill the oxygen bottle with distilled water; wash the kitchen
    floor.

that's any day (except for the kitchen floor, which is any
one day in 1986). on particular days I have other things to do:

write my parents; write Tim Robbins in Bloomington;
    clear off
my desk & write any letters that go along with that (turn
down

the Chancellor's annual fall picnic invitation). & special
    things:
talk seriously with John's father about preparations; call the

obituary writer at the *Globe* to find out what to do when
    the time comes;
water the plants again; & give some time to my private
    vices,

without which I would have collapsed in July. (watch a
    baseball
game, for a moderate instance.) I'm still tired, but I figure
    I can

last the distance, as they say about running, even though I'm
only staying at home & going to work & therapy & trying
    to make time

as rich as I can in this immobile place.

"recoveries" (9-8-86)

John said to me a few days ago, "I didn't know it could be this good." He was talking about the way I was caring for him, and at first I took it as pure compliment. But he also meant: "I didn't realize a man could be this caring." In his own family and in his friendships John is far more intimate with women, whom he prefers and whom he tends to trust, than he is with men.

Most of John's energy is now reserved for visitors, especially his family. When they leave John here at home, they go away—in their distress—to pray for a miracle for John. Maybe his animation with them suggests that he may recover; with his family he tries to disguise his pain.

Sunday Richie, John's brother, and his father came together to visit. It was the only time that Richie visited his brother. I was two rooms away while they talked, or rather while John talked and they provided occasional comments. There had been a rift between Richie and his father, and John was trying to bring the whole family back together before he died. After they left, John was pleased; he said he had accomplished what he tried to do.

My emotions, though, were mixed. John is always exhausted after a weekend of visits, and this time John's father and brother had let John do nearly all the emotional work. He would be deeply exhausted now. He would sleep a long night and much of the next day.

9-12-86

John's lost more weight.
yesterday he was incontinent

& ashamed of it. he's
sleeping even more. then

Wednesday he seemed better.
he talked more. & yes-

terday he ate fried rice
& coffee ice cream, his

first food in three weeks.
he'd been dehydrated &

very weak. he's still
probably dehydrated & weak,

but he's not dead.
Lisa says she's never seen it

like this before, or seen
the like of his pure will,

which is all he's living on.
I knew he was strong, but

it's all spirit now, his body
down to a persistent wraith,

his eyes shining.

microcosm (9-13-86)

he's awake at night, reading.
at 8 a.m., one hour past

pill time, he's still asleep.
his hours are his own,

nothing to do with the clock,
except when visitors come.

''he's content in that small
room,'' Lisa says, without

walking, without leaving it.
: dog, fish, flowers, books,

television; pills, urinal,
bedpan. a whole world here,

& he's already lived longer
than anyone thought.

9-17-86

Saturday Jack told me
his therapist was dying.

Mauricio—married now,
with one son—died Saturday

night; I'll go to his memorial
service today. yesterday

Paul Fowler was diagnosed;
I called him in the hospital,

where he feels good. Bob
Johnson died (that's why we

have Lisa 8 hours a day
instead of 5). & John

is still living: Monday

night fried clams & butter-
scotch pudding. Barbara

—on vacation in Italy for
two weeks—thinks John will

still be alive when she gets
back. Lisa & I don't think so,

but it's all baffling.
"what do we know?" we ask

each other. while outside
it closes in, raw weather.

cold rain.

closing in (9-23-86)

Mauricio Gaston, 39.
Lisa's last two patients

were both stronger than
John is now when they died,

& John stays in bed &
lives. yesterday he lost

all feeling in his legs &
called to me. I helped him

bend his knees. "not yet,"
he says, he wants to talk

with everyone, to tell them
how much they mean to him.

Jim Everhard, this summer in
DC. John hangs on.

now they've released AZT
& I've been to Mass General

three days running. it will
be too late, or John will

have to go in for tests to
please the regulators, &

he can't. three months ago
he might have had more time.

he's still living, with little
to live *on*. it's September,

already the fall. the days
get shorter. he might have

made it, but he won't.

pain (9-23-86)

compared with cancer, the
pain is not great. but it's

real—in the legs, which went
numb last night; in my own

head when John cries out in pain.
I give him codeine & it helps.

we have 100 at a time now,
a prescription I could not

get filled at Phillips, where
the pharmacist treated me like

a strung-out junky with a
fake form. but I am strung out

only with pain & worry.
I give him morphine, which

helps him sleep, till he
awakens in pain, & I get up

to give him codeine &
morphine again.

9-25-86

it's been good for him, this
cocoon of dog, fish, books,

flowering plants. but I'm
frightened. "What are you

afraid of?" my therapist asks me.
"of his dying," I say.

just that. I don't know why.
I'm not unhappy yet, just scared.

he'll die soon. not tonight,
probably not tomorrow. I've

made tomorrow's list: get
dilantin, phenolbarbitol,

write obituary; get pictures
developed for those who are

still alive to see them.

weather forecast (10-3-86)

"it will get quite darker
this afternoon, with a

partial eclipse of the sun."
but it will (has) also rain(ed)

so the eclipse, partial to
begin with, could not be seen.

it rained hard.
—good for the soil, but

tomorrow (& tonight), it will
get colder, this Indian summer

gone sooner than we expected.
& next week a cold front is

coming in from Canada.
I can only anticipate change.

I'll feel relief, but the center
of my life will be utterly

removed, the way one cores
an apple before eating the fruit.

deathwatch 2 (10-5-86)

John is sleeping.
Lisa is rubbing his legs.

when she doesn't rub them,
they get cold. fast.

his pulse is faster—
like his heartbeat yesterday

when Barbara listened to it.
Nancy & Bobby are coming, a

last visit. Donny—who
grew up with John, was like a

brother with him (more than
his own brother), just called;

he'd heard the end was close.
it's very close. we're waiting.

10-6-86

John's awake. I heard his
cough, but he's calm.

"can I get you anything?"
he shakes his head. "I've

turned on the light in my
aquarium in the living room."

John smiles. he doesn't
say anything. Saturday his

father; yesterday Nancy &
Bobby. it's all been

completed, very well.
last night he said,

"everyone loves me."
there is nothing really

left for John & me to do.
but we talked. he's calm,

peaceful. he's ready now.
one year ago tonight Peter's

mother died. an anniversary.
this is another year.

10-7-86

"how do you feel?
do you feel calm?"

I ask. "I feel sick,"
John says. "oh," I say

& go back to my room
to play another game

of solitaire.
oh, and oh and oh.

I don't know what to do
but wait for Lisa to come

at 8 or 8:15, but wait
for it all finally

to be over, for that
huge hole to open in the

middle of my life, where
I've been filled for

years and months now,
to the very brim.

10-8-86

when John woke up, dis-
oriented, he said, ''it was

beautiful''—not like the
last dream before he was

ready. when he's sleeping
there's a look of peace on

his face, &, sometimes,
when he talks (softly now),

he says he is happy.
he knows he is loved;

he loves me & the others.
he's ready now.

in my dream two nights ago
I decided not to try AZT.

when I phoned Chip Schooley,
he called that ''a wise decision.''

I'm ready too, then, for
John to die. after that

I don't know anything.

10-9-86

yesterday he was awake,
this morning awake. he

barely talks. his body
is so shrunken that it

hurts him to move at all;
his flesh is gone. why

does he hang on? three days
ago he spoke about how

happy he was, everything
resolved, the people who

love him, those he loves,
including his father.

when he slept the expression
on his face was peaceful.

now it's a frown. have things
got unresolved? not with

me or Lisa; we are past
"ready" now & he's at ease

with us. & I have no peace
at all: at work I think

about him, at home, when I
worry about moving the plants

indoors before Friday's cold.
& John hangs on, restless but

immobile, his eyes
staring into space.

do I want him to be dead? (10-13-86)

not *be* dead, but—maybe—
finally, to die. can I admit

that to myself? is it what
I want? how else explain my

anger last night at Suzanne,
Bobby, & Nancy, who smiled

that John wanted a pizza &
assumed that I'd go out to

get it (though my leg ached,
though I was exhausted; &

Bobby drove to get it).
I haven't climbed a mountain;

John's done that, but the
mountain has climbed me.

the treat people & the care people (10-13-86)

the care people are tired.
one of them—Lisa—has got

a second wind. another
—Ron—is still winded; he

aches all over. but the
treat people come & smile.

John gets alert for them.
yesterday he even drank

Ensure again & demanded—
just as three of them were

leaving—a pizza. he ate
one slice: first food in

three weeks. when the
care people give up, the

treat people hang right
in there. they smile &

talk & John smiles &
talks back.

the treat people & the care people (2)

"John's eating," they say. but
I frown, imitating John. "he's

not gaining weight any more,"
I tell them. "but he's eating,"

they rejoice, "he's keeping it
down." then the treat people go

home. I'm already home. I give
John a morphine suppository

when they leave (for he's in pain,
which he denied when they were here).

later, in the middle of the night,
I give him another suppository, but

this time I have to get rid of the
pellets of shit that come out (the

results of his eating, the only
results) so the morphine is

absorbed & he won't scream out in pain
again for hours.

10-25-86

Since Wednesday John has been in tremendous pain. The bed sores, which had already begun to form all over his body, have grown worse, and one must be careful to place him in such a way that they are not exacerbated. Sometimes pillows or rolled up towels must be placed where the flesh is nearly gone and only bone protrudes. Sometimes the sores start to bleed.

I want him to die now. The most difficult thing, all along, is to see John in pain and be able to do nothing to help him. When we move him, he screams. Only when his family comes, or maybe Suzanne, does he try to put a good face on things. He's cheerful, he talks and even laughs. When Nancy and Joanne and Suzanne left Wednesday, John told me he felt better. But five minutes later he asked for a morphine suppository and two codeine tablets.

Last night I called his parents so his mother could come today. He asked for her. Besides, she is trained as a home health aide and knows how to move him. He is supposed to be moved every two hours. Except, by the time Lisa left at four yesterday afternoon, John had begun to sleep. I did not give him his pills last night at seven because he was still sleeping. He is breathing very deeply, relatively short deep breaths. He is still asleep at six in the morning. He is still breathing deeply, and he has not awakened yet.

still alive (10-25-86)

he slept through the night:
four to eight—no pain

when he sleeps. I slept:
eight to eleven; eleven

to three; three to four;
up at six. worked.

typed two documents,
played solitaire. mailed

letters at the corner
store,where I got cig-

arettes but no paper
(they didn't have one).

came back. played soli-
taire. till John screamed

just now, & I gave him
a morphine capsule.

he's on his stomach.
wet? I don't know; I

didn't turn him over.
I love you, he said.

I'd said that to him
first, and—let it go now;

I'm all right. I *am*
all right, whatever

that means. it means
ready. & I told him so

& he understands me. it's
time for the others to

tell him too.

10-29-86

I tried, last weekend, to convince John's sister Nancy and his parents John & Lucille to give John the space & the encouragement to die. With Nancy it was clear; she could not wish it. His father said, "We don't think that way. It's God's will." "Fine," I said, "but let John know that you accept it either way." No luck. I lost the argument.

I did convince his mother to come both weekend days. I was glad Lisa was not available. When I was out on errands Saturday morning, a decision was made to which I was asked to acquiesce: that John would go home with his mother (to his mother) in Holbrook. "That's what John wants," they said. And "we had been thinking about it, but we didn't want to say anything until Johnny said something." Not to me either, who had no notion what they had been thinking about. (The house queer; the house nigger. He's done his job —back to the family into which John was born.)

How could I tell what John wanted. He has been alert these last three weeks only for visitors. To Lisa he says, "I want to die." Sometimes that's what he says to me. Friday night he slept 16 hours. 20 hours Sunday night, when his family had gone.

Tuesday morning John was alert and I was able to determine that he does want to go. The result is OK with me. We've done our closure really. We love each other.

It's Wednesday now, 9:30. His parents will be here soon. Lisa is here now. Gail has just arrived. I'm doing a laundry. The ambulance is coming at 11 to take John to his parents' home.

leaving (10-29-86)

Lisa & I were here.
his parents arrived,

his father worried
but excited, that silly

characteristic grin,
his son coming home for

a miracle. no idea
what's going on, his

mother doesn't know either.
when the ambulance men come,

I can't watch but go down-
stairs to hold the doors

open. & John comes down
on the stretcher, again.

when they open the ambulance
doors & put John inside,

he looks at me & three times
screams my name. then

his mother gets inside,
they close the doors,

& he's gone.

the next day (10-30-86)

Lisa & I went back upstairs
& stripped the bed, half-

heartedly cleaned the room,
throwing away some things,

piling up others. I went
downstairs to do John's laundry

the last time (sometimes I'd
done 3 or 4 laundries in a

day, however many times he
needed clean bedding). Lisa

stayed a while (we need each
other now, we'll miss each

other), then she left.
today I potted geraniums

for the winter since it may
freeze tonight.

the birds of sorrow (11-1-86)

have almost all migrated
now, the Canada geese a

roar of noise, the hawks stopping
over the Cape. all gone

South like the satyrs,
their yellow & black wings

a whoosh of noise. *we
cannot prevent,* the Chinese

sage says (in the passage
my mother sent me from Florida)

*the birds of sorrow from
flying over our heads.*

I put on my winter clothing
—T-shirt, flannel shirt—

as the weather changes.
but we can refuse (against

the cold come suddenly into
my body now John is gone)

to let them build nests
(my cats protect me; eyeing

the birds; salivating)
in our hair.

6 a.m. disoriented (11-3-86)

normally at this time
I'm just getting up,

listening for sounds
from John—a glass

shattering, his calling me
—knowing that Lisa

will be here in two hours,
more or less. normally

I'm hoping to hear nothing,
to get on with my work

(whatever that is), but
all that's changed.

John isn't here—he's
with his parents pre-

paring to die. Lisa isn't
coming. & the way I used to live

isn't normal anymore. what's
left is just the cats, &

they matter, & two extra
fish tanks I don't even want,

but we didn't know how to move
fish in the ambulance that

took John away.

November 5, 1986
(1:45 p.m.)

in his sleep.
quietly.

no more pain.
I guess I was

the last one to
speak with him,

yesterday afternoon,
though Nancy went in

just after I left,
but then John fell

asleep. & kept
sleeping.

& died.

11-5-86

I was in the middle of a meeting. It was 3:30. Mary Lind appeared at the door; someone called my attention to her. I got up, quickly, asked Vivian to take notes for me, and I left. When I got back to my office, I didn't have his family's phone number, so I called information. Then called the number. First his mother answered: John died at a quarter to two, she said.

I drove home, got the obituary and the power of attorney form and drove to the Boston *Globe*. Bobby's name can't go in—no in-laws; neither can Joanne's—no aunts; not Suzanne's—only one friend. The immediate family + Ron. The young man, who was kind and seemed to know his job, wanted more information about John's job. I suggested that he call Winston's. But I called Winston's and asked Maynard if he knew. Maynard thought I was talking about John's move to Holbrook; he didn't know. So I told him.

Then I asked Maynard whether he could talk, and he could. I left the *Globe*; Maynard could give the young man, whose name is John, more information about John's work.

I drove back to my office and tried to make phone calls. I got through to my parents and to Alba. I left a message for Barbara at Hospice, for Gail on the answering machine. I couldn't get through to Tom & Russ or to Larry, or to Lisa. I decided not to tell Suzanne until I went home. And then, later, I was able to reach Lisa as well.

I went to therapy and Richard helped. I went to my men's group, and Milt, David, Dick, Peter, Mark and Jim helped.

But maybe there is no help. Not now. I don't like it.

how did it end?

when they carried John out of the
house (on his way to Holbrook) he

looked up at me as they put him in
the ambulance & screamed "Ron! Ron!

Ron!" then they closed the doors,
his mother with him, & drove off.

what happened next?

John went to Holbrook, where they
set him up in a hospital bed. on

Thursday I visited. the nurse
asked me to help her turn John over,

though his mother was there, & trained,
as I was not. by Saturday his mother

was less helpless, more in charge.
his father was pleased to have John

(who was not queer, who had acknowledged
Jesus) home & smiling at him.

what else happened?

Wednesday morning, before his family
arrived to take him "home," John said

to Lisa: "look after Ron because my
family surely won't."

how did it end?

I visited the third time on Tuesday,
& spoke with John. when I left the

room to drive home, Nancy went in,
but John had already fallen asleep.

how did it end (2)?

I wasn't there. twice before
—when John was home with me—

he'd slept a long time: 16
hours, 20 hours. the second time

I'd called Lisa—how do I know
if he's died? I asked. & she told me.

I was at a meeting when the call came.
Mary, my secretary, came in & signaled

to me. I knew what it was.

Gail was there. his mother was there.
John had not awakened but Gail was

talking to him. "I have to go in
ten minutes," Gail said. & then

John's hand went limp as she held it.
John's mother did not realize, though

she held his other hand. "he's gone,"
Gail said. & he is.

John MacDonald Jr. Floral designer in Boston, 35

CAMBRIDGE – John W. MacDonald Jr., a floral designer in Boston for several years, died Wednesday in his home after a long illness. He was 35.

Mr. MacDonald for the past 11 years was a floral designer at Winston Flowers in Boston.

He designed the arrangements for the 100th anniversary celebration of the Boston Pops, Kevin White's last two mayoral inaugurations, and many other functions throughout the city and state.

Mr. MacDonald was born in Dorchester and had been living in Cambridge for the past seven years.

He graduated from Holbrook High School and attended Northeastern University before transferring to the University of Hawaii, from which he received a bachelor's degree in marine biology.

Mr. MacDonald is survived by his parents, John and Lucille (Gagne) MacDonald of Holbrook; two sisters, Nancy Peter of West Bridgewater and Christine MacDonald of Holbrook; a brother, Richard MacDonald of Milton; and an aunt, Joanne MacDonald of Randolph.

A memorial service will be held at 1 p.m. Monday, Nov. 10, in Brookville Baptist Church in Holbrook. Interment will be private.

—The Boston Globe

John W. MacDonald Jr.

CAMBRIDGE, MA — John W. MacDonald, Jr., died Wednesday, November 5, in his home here. John had AIDS and had been bedridden since April. He was 35 years old.

John worked for the past 11 years at Winston Flowers on Newbury Street. He designed the arrangements for the 100th anniversary celebration of the Boston Pops and for many other functions held across the city and state.

John is survived by his lover of nine years, Ron Schreiber, by his friend and roommate Suzanne Meglio, and by his family. (An obituary appeared in the Boston *Globe* November 7, but mention of his lover was omitted by order of John's father.)

—Gay Community News